Basic Helps
to
Confession

Fr Bill

ST PAULS

Original English edition title : *Basic Helps to Confession*
by Fr Bill Murphy

Copyright © 2000, Daughters of St Paul

Nihil Obstat: Rev John J. Connelly, STD
Imprimatur: †Bernard Cardinal Law
Archbishop of Boston
April 11, 2000

ST PAULS Publishing
187 Battersea Bridge Road, London SW11 3AS, UK
www.stpauls.ie

First published in UK 2001

ISBN 085439 619 5

Set by TuKan DTP, Fareham, Hampshire, UK
Printed by AGAM, Cuneo, Italy

ST PAULS is an activity of the priests and brothers
of the Society of St Paul who proclaim the Gospel
through the media of social communication

**'Come to me,
all you who are weary and
find life burdensome,
and I will refresh you.'**

(Mt 11:28)

If you have picked up this pamphlet you have a reason to be interested in the sacrament of Reconciliation of the Catholic Church. What is this mysterious ritual about? What does it accomplish? What goes on within the private exchange between a priest and a member of the Church?

Perhaps you are exploring the possibility of becoming a Catholic.

Perhaps you were baptised a Catholic but not instructed in the faith when you were younger. It may be that you are preparing for the sacrament of Confirmation, Marriage, or the Baptism of your child and wish to learn more about forgiveness and reconciliation. Whatever the reason, any time is a good time to explore the gift God has given to the Church in the sacrament of Reconciliation. With some reading and personal reflection, you may witness a new horizon of freedom opening before you. The sacrament of Reconciliation is meant to offer just that: richer relationships, a greater appreciation of God, and a more complete experience of life through forgiveness of sin. Let's get started.

What Exactly is this Sacrament Called?

This sacrament seems to have more names than any other sacrament of the Church. Even the *Catechism of the Catholic Church*, the official summary of Church teaching, offers several: conversion, penance, confession, forgiveness, and reconciliation (cf. *CCC*, 1423-1424). Don't worry about using the 'right' name for it. The people with whom you worship probably use one or another of the most common terms: sacrament of Reconciliation or the sacrament of Penance. Many Catholics, by habit, refer to 'going to Confession'. Each of the available names says something important about the sacrament.

• **Conversion**, which means 'to turn completely', describes a movement that takes place inside us. When a Christian becomes aware of damage done to a relationship, whether with God or another person, the first sign of hope is a desire to turn away from that behaviour and toward a deeper life in Christ. A conversion is a complete turning, where a failed behaviour or outlook is put aside and a new way is sought. The sacrament proclaims and celebrates this inner spiritual movement.

• **Penance** is an action undertaken to repair or show sorrow for wrongdoing. It is a demonstration to God, to oneself, and to those who may have been hurt that real change is beginning to take place. Sometimes a person who apologises much but changes little is told, 'I'll believe it when I see it.' Penance is action that helps to turn a desire to change into a reality.

• **Confession** is the telling of sins. In the case of the sacrament, sins are told to a priest. The priest has no personal interest in the sins of others, but listens because it is good for the soul to say out loud to some one what we have done. To use images, confession cleanses the soul and lifts the burden of guilt. Confession gets the burden 'off our chest'.

• **Forgiveness** is what we seek. Jesus Christ's death on the cross has brought the reality of forgiveness of sins to every created soul; through Christ, we have been 'set right' with God. But our sins damage that harmonious relationship. To restore it, we must seek from God a renewal of forgiveness. God freely for gives our sins. We prove our sincerity by the actions we take: apology and reparation.

• **Reconciliation** is the action of unity once more being experienced among separated persons. Friends, spouses, relatives, co-workers or acquaintances who have been divided by misunderstanding, fear, or offence, find relief and even deep joy in drawing close once more. Because God is the source of all healing love, God is always present when reconciliation occurs. Our relationship with God and the Church, as well as with those we may have hurt, is renewed and strengthened through reconciliation.

Each of the terms used in the *Catechism* sheds light on a different value given to us by God in this sacrament. As becomes obvious, using this sacrament is much more than a routine religious practice. It is a useful, practical way of keeping our relationship with God and others strong. It is an essential tool for keeping relationships centred in Christian faith.

One Sacrament, Four Parts

In order to receive God's forgiveness through this sacrament, the penitent (the one making the confession) and the priest complete four steps:

• The first is *confession*. It is necessary for the penitent to tell his or her sins to the priest. This is done privately, and the priest is *never* allowed to refer to those sins, to anyone. This absolute confidentiality allows the penitent to reveal all sources of shame and guilt without worrying that they will be revealed.

• The second part is *contrition*. Contrition means sorrow. In some way, usually by a memorised prayer, the penitent tells the priest that he or she is truly sorry for having committed these sins and will make every effort not to repeat them. If a person is not sorry there is no point in seeking forgiveness.

• The third step is *penance*. The priest asks the penitent to perform some spiritual or charitable work. As mentioned above, the purpose of penance is to begin the work of change. The penance is completed after the penitent departs from the priest.

• The final step is *absolution*. The priest prays a specific prayer over the penitent. These beautiful words summarise God's loving work through Christ. They also, through the power of the Holy Spirit, release the soul of the penitent from the burden of sin. As far as God is concerned, the sin disappears from history.

Why Must I Tell My Sins to a Priest?

Maybe you have asked yourself this question or have heard it discussed among others. People will say, 'God is everywhere. God knows my heart and God knows my sorrow. Why can't I receive God's forgiveness through my private prayer? Why should I tell another person?' Even those who have made use of this sacrament for years, sometimes wish that they could avoid speaking to a priest. Admitting our sins is hard – we simply don't like to embarrass ourselves! So, why do we have to?

It's true that God is everywhere and knows us. God knows us better than we know ourselves. God is also eager to forgive us and to welcome us into a life of deeper love and faithfulness. But the Church, based on the words of Jesus Christ, requires that sins be confessed to a priest for the sacramental forgiveness to take place.

Jesus knows well that we human beings need encouragement to face our problems and responsibilities. Christ knows that we are easily ashamed of our mistakes and would prefer to hide them away. He also knows that our hidden mistakes are never removed if no one can get at them. So, the Risen Lord Jesus gave to his Apostles a share in his ministry of reconciliation. Jesus Christ wanted others to be able to help those who sin with the same generous love and understanding he displayed in his ministry. So, after he rose from the dead, Jesus '...breathed on [the Apostles] and said to them, "Receive the Holy Spirit. If you forgive the sins of any, they are forgiven them; if you retain the sins of any, they are retained"' (Jn 20:22b-23). As with all the sacraments, an action of Christ is the source of this one. Jesus has invited others, representing himself, to share in the careful work of bringing God's healing love to the pain of sin and guilt.

There is obvious wisdom in Christ's involving another person (the priest) in our forgiveness. God desires our healing to be a fully human one and so it must involve another person, because our sins have hurt others. The structure of sacramental confession makes us give voice to our sins. That means we have to think carefully about our lives and speak our sins out loud. This forces us to take responsibility. It helps us to appreciate the damage we have done by our actions. It is not that God wants us to feel awful about ourselves. Rather, God wants us to be realistic so that we can seek and accept a healing that matches the injury.

Another value found in sacramental confession is the response given by the priest. The priest is expected to listen carefully and respond to the penitent with mature and fitting guidance. We cannot give ourselves such advice. Nor does God ordinarily do so, except through others.

Still another benefit in bringing our sins to the sacrament is in the penance we are given. The priest asks us to fulfil some work of prayer, charity, or reparation to help to make up for what we have done. This is an assignment that must be completed before the forgiveness takes effect. If it were only up to us, we might never assign ourselves such as task. The sacrament of Penance provides a structure where we find what we need in order to seek and to experience God's mercy in the fullest possible way.

So, what seems to be an embarrassing requirement is, actually, a carefully structured method designed by God that will bring us a rich experience and valuable insight. There God goes again, doing things for our own good!

Deciding What to Confess

Most of the time we approach this sacrament knowing what to confess. Through feelings of guilt, our heart tells us our faults. We have a good sense of how we have not met the standards by which we hope to live. Our sins stand out because we feel ashamed. However, our guilty feelings do not always provide a complete and accurate account. In some cases, we are unaware of the damage caused by certain actions. In other cases, we may feel overly guilty for something insignificant. We humans can get kind of weird about guilt sometimes. Here the Church helps us to relax. The Church reaches into its vast experience to help us separate the guilt of sin from other bad feelings. Therefore, it is helpful to consider our lives according to guidelines given to us by God through the Church. The idea behind such guidelines is to see clearly.

Before taking a look at our behaviour, we need a clear definition of sin. Sin is not only something that makes us feel bad or ashamed, but it is a harmful action that is done intentionally and with the knowledge that it is wrong.

It may be directed toward another person, the Church or society at large, or God. The *Catechism of the Catholic Church* repeats a centuries-old formula describing two kinds of sin: *mortal* and *venial*. A mortal sin turns a person completely away from God. God is refused, blocked off. Such an act can only be committed with full knowledge and deliberate consent. We must know what we are doing, and mean to do it. Also, it must clearly be wrong, for example, the breaking of one of the Ten Commandments (cf. *CCC*, nos. 1855, 1857). A venial sin is less serious, either because the damage is less severe or because it is done in partial ignorance or without complete freedom (cf. *CCC*, no. 1862). With venial sins, we may be only partly aware the act is wrong, or perhaps we felt pressured or backed into a corner.

There are times when 'venial' or lesser sins are the only ones on our consciences. In these cases, the Church recognises that God's forgiveness may be received without the sacrament of Reconciliation. How? By God's mercy, which is always active and available to us. Through a clear understanding of what the sins are, together with a sincere desire to change, less serious sins are forgiven. In these cases, a good way to express sorrow is praying an Act of Contrition or participating thoughtfully in the Penitential Rite at the beginning of the Eucharistic Celebration.

Even if you are not aware of having committed mortal sin, it is good not to remain too long without receiving the sacrament of Reconciliation. The Church requires that each member of the Church confess any mortal sin at least once a year (cf. *Code of Canon Law*, no. 989). Also, if we are aware of mortal sin, we are not to receive Holy Communion without first receiving the sacrament of Reconciliation (cf. *Code of Canon Law*, no. 916). But beyond these rules, the Church encourages frequent use of this sacrament. Regular self-examination, confession, and penance help us to stay close to God and one another. Going to confession once a month is not too often. The sacrament of Reconciliation is a healing encounter with God the Father, Son, and Holy Spirit. Practised responsibly by both penitent and priest, it is always a good thing.

Examining One's Conscience

What is the 'conscience'? In the Walt Disney version of *Pinocchio*, the enchanted puppet has a companion, a cricket, which tries to warn Pinocchio of danger and keep him from bad and foolish behaviour. Jiminy Cricket represents Pinocchio's conscience. I recently heard someone describe conscience as 'God's e-mail' – messages from God to help us understand God's will.

The Church's understanding of conscience requires neither insects nor computer programs. It is a natural part of every person. Conscience is the name we give to a kind of inner voice, which speaks without words. It leads us toward good and away from evil. Conscience also makes judgements about that which we have already done. It is a sacred part of each person, given to us by God, helping us to know how to follow Christ faithfully.

An important part of preparing for the sacrament of Reconciliation is an 'examination of conscience'. During this exercise, the penitent sets time aside to think and to pray. The main question to ask ourselves is: how well have I been living as a disciple of Jesus Christ, and where have I failed?

Sometimes, we can answer this question immediately. There will be obvious examples of failure. Each of us has long-established patterns of weakness. We find ourselves making the same mistakes and committing the same sins repeatedly, the 'old standbys' that keep us awake at night. But there are also more subtle ways in which we stray from Christ's example. Sin hides well. By looking at ourselves carefully, though, we may discover the unexpected sins in our lives. We may even be able to see patterns of sin that we did not recognise before. Clarity is the purpose of examining one's conscience. By seeing more clearly, we are better able to seek the help we need. By seeking help, we become freer in our drawing closer to God.

Getting Down to Business

So far, we have seen why the Church requires Catholics to make use of the sacrament of Reconciliation, and what we mean by 'sin'. Now, we need a way of identifying and understanding our own sins. To move toward this, first pray to God for clarity. Ask God to help you to see and accept the particular sins for which you are responsible. Then explore your behaviour since your last confession. Various guide lines are helpful. The Beatitudes (cf. Mt 5), St Paul's list of the works of the flesh (cf. Gal 5:19-21), or the Seven Deadly Sins (pride, anger, lust, greed, sloth, gluttony, envy) provide useful structures. Here we will use a common method: examining oneself through reflection on the Ten Commandments. The commandments are listed below in bold type. Under each commandment are questions for reflection. These are not official questions provided by the Church, but I offer them here to help you focus your thoughts as you look over your life. They are not essay questions, just ways of jogging your mind and heart. If they are helpful to you, I am glad. If you find other ways to come to a deeper understanding of your own behaviour, that is fine, too. If these questions make it difficult for you to examine your conscience, feel free to choose another path. How you go about examining your life is not as important as doing it carefully. Let's begin.

I
I am the Lord your God;
you shall not have strange gods before me

Is a desire for God part of your daily activities? Do you let other desires interfere with knowing, loving, and serving God? Do you doubt the existence of God? Do you doubt God's love for you? Do you encourage spiritual doubt in others? Have you boasted of sin? Have you let love of material goods, physical pleasures, or personal status determine your choices? Do you believe you do not need God? Do you believe you must earn God's love? Are you angry with God? Have you refused to ask questions about God or the faith out of fear of being wrong? Do you pray regularly? Have you dismissed as unimportant any teaching of Christ or the Church? Have you broken promises or vows made to God? Do you try to develop your conscience through prayer, study, and questioning? Have you sought control over your life through superstition, magic, witchcraft, or those who claim to possess psychic powers? Have you prayed for the intercession of the saints for selfish things? Have you prayed that harm might come to someone?

II
You shall not take the name of the Lord your God in vain

Have you used the name of God as a curse or exclamation? Have you used the name of God, Jesus Christ, the Virgin Mary, or the saints in a way that detracts from faith or offends others? Have you made a promise in God's name without a strong intention to keep it? Have you used the name of God to coerce others to do your will? Have you sworn a false oath or lied, using God's name to prove your sincerity?

III
Remember the Sabbath day, to keep it holy

Have you attended Mass on Sundays and Holy Days of Obligation? Have you gone to Church for some purpose other than the worship of God (e.g. meeting people, looking good to your neighbours)? Have you distracted others from their worship? Do you participate in the Christian community and bring support, encouragement, and strength to your parish? Do you allow yourself time for reflection, restoration and the growth of your spiritual life? Do you make a time of rest for yourself and those for whom you are responsible?

IV
Honour your father and your mother

Have you shown due love, kindness, respect, and compassion to your parents? Have you made an effort to understand them in times of disagreement? Do you pray for them? Are you willing to give encouragement and material assistance to your parents? Are you respectful of all your family members, recognising the bond you share? Do you show respect and due obedience to those in authority over you? Are you conscientious regarding your duties as a citizen? Do you support laws and public policies that strengthen the family? Are you respectful of all persons, no matter how close or distant the relationship?

V
You shall not kill

Have you taken the life of another, or caused another to die? Have you participated in the act of abortion, infanticide, or euthanasia? Have you encouraged or enabled another to do so? Have you failed to relieve the suffering of others where possible? Have you endangered the safety of others through the abuse of alcohol, drugs, or through the reckless use of vehicles? Have you held hatred for another person? Have you encouraged others to reject the goodness of another person? Have you wilfully damaged the reputation of another? Have you ridiculed or insulted others? Have you spread prejudicial ideas concerning persons of a particular racial, ethnic, religious, economic, or other grouping? Do you respect yourself as one loved deeply by God? Do you respect your health and avoid excesses of physical neglect or obsession? Have you led others into the practice of any sin? Do you support movements within society that protect life, promote peace, and encourage tolerance?

VI
You shall not commit adultery

Do you accept the goodness of sexuality, for yourself and others? Do you respect the sanctity of marriage? Have you encouraged others to be drawn away from the Christian understanding of marital commitment? Do you accept the value of chastity for all unmarried persons? Have you engaged in sexual activity with someone other than your spouse? Do you intentionally prevent the conception of children by artificial means?

VII
You shall not steal

Have you taken possession of something that did not belong to you? Have you done damage to the property of another? Have you withheld money or property that is owed to another? Have you caused others to pay excessively for goods or services? Have you cheated another out of property, money, or rights? Have you gambled so as to risk being unable to provide for yourself or others? Do you show respect for the natural world and make efforts to conserve its resources for future generations? Do you promote fair labour practices and just compensation? Do you give to the poor?

VIII
You shall not bear false witness against your neighbour

Have you lied? Have you committed perjury by lying under oath? Have you damaged the reputation of another? Have you revealed negative facts about another without proper reason? Do you discuss the affairs of others? Have you allowed another person to continue doing something wrong? Have you revealed secrets that have been told to you? Have you broken a professional standard of confidentiality in the workplace?

IX
You shall not covet your neighbour's wife

Do you lust after the spouse of another? Do you nurse feelings of sexual desire for someone who is not your spouse? Do you express lustful thoughts in the company of others? Are you careless about where you look, what you say, and what you do regarding sexual behaviour? Do you use sexualised speech? Do you touch others or make gestures to satisfy sexual feelings? Do you go to places that deal in sexual material or behaviour for the purpose of becoming aroused? Do you use pornography? Do you masturbate? Have you failed to protect the sexual innocence of children? Do you see sexual activity as a cure for loneliness? Do you appreciate the dignity of every person? Do you see the value of your own sexual integrity?

X
You shall not covet your neighbour's goods

Do you often wish you had what another has? Are you greedy, desiring more than you need? Do you have a desire to amass wealth and possessions without limit? Do you feel envious, becoming sad or frustrated at another's happiness or success? Do you wish harm or failure to someone who is more successful than you? Have you caused tension or disagreement by insisting unreasonably on receiving a certain portion of goods? Do you wish misfortune to another so that you will somehow profit? Do you seek the power that may accompany wealth?

One final question: *Are you willing to forgive yourself with the same generosity God has in forgiving you?*

Okay, It's Time

When you have reflected on the presence of sin in your life, and have identified those sins which you have committed since the last time you went to confession, give thanks to God for God's guidance and contact a priest.

Most parishes have scheduled times for the sacrament. Often they are on Saturday afternoon, prior to the first Eucharistic Celebration of the weekend. You may always telephone the rectory and set up an appointment with a priest for another time, if that is more convenient.

It was mentioned earlier that the celebration of this sacrament is a private matter. Prior to the updating of this ritual in the 1970s, almost every confession was heard in a 'confessional box'. The priest sat in a small dark compartment. The penitent entered a similarly darkened space attached to the priest's box. The penitent knelt down and the conversation took place through a screen. In this way, the priest did not know the penitent's identity. Many parishes and shrines still make this style available.

When the ritual was revised, an option to meet the priest face to face was established. Many parishes have built a special room for the celebration of the sacrament. In this room, the penitent may still kneel before a screen, preserving anonymity. Or the penitent may walk around the screen and sit across from the priest. If you are going to meet with the priest by appointment and wish not to be known, this may be arranged, too. You'll have to discuss how when you call.

When you and the priest are ready, make the sign of the cross. Then tell the priest how long it has been since your last confession or if this is your first one. Tell the priest your sins. Listen carefully to his comments. Ask for clarification if you need it. Make sure you understand the penance he gives you. The penance should be both reasonable and possible to complete. If you feel the penance is too difficult or for some other reason you cannot fulfil it, please let the priest know.

Pray aloud an Act of Contrition or words of your own choosing which express your sorrow and resolution to change. Listen to the priest as he prays the words of absolution. Through God's power and mercy, these words lift the burden of sin from your soul.

Complete the penance you have been given as soon as possible. Your efforts to live humbly and honestly in God's presence will surely be blessed.

An Act of Contrition

Loving God, Heavenly Father,
I have sinned against you
and against persons I should love.
I am sorry for my sins.
By your grace,
poured out through the sacrifice of the cross,
forgive my sins.
I promise to live more faithfully as your child,
avoiding these and all sins.
Amen.

A Practical Summary of Celebrating the Sacrament of Penance

- Find out where and when the sacrament is celebrated in your parish or make an appointment to meet privately with a priest.
- Understand clearly how your behaviour has damaged your relationship with God, the Church, and persons in your life.
- Begin with a Sign of the Cross and tell the priest how long it has been since your last confession.
- Tell the priest your sins.
- Listen for any words from him which may help you to deepen your faithfulness to Christ and avoid repeating the sins.
- When the priest gives you a penance, indicate you understand it, or ask for clarification if you don't.
- Say an Act of Contrition (one is suggested on page 29).
- Listen to the words of absolution.
- Complete your penance.
- Thank God for this great moment of grace in your life!

ABOUT THE AUTHOR

A native of Boston, Massachusetts, Rev Bill Murphy graduated from Emerson College in Boston and then entered St John's Seminary in Brighton. He was ordained for service to the Archdiocese of Boston in 1988. Fr Murphy has served in two parish assignments and has also worked in the area of clergy personnel. He is currently serving as a spiritual director at St John's Seminary.